KEEPING CHRISTMAS

KEEPING CHRISTMAS

An Edwardian-Age Memoir

by WILLIAM F. STRICKER

Illustrated by
JOSEPH SHEPPARD

Stemmer
House
PUBLISHERS, INC.
OWINGS MILLS, MARYLAND

Inquiries should be directed to
Stemmer House Publishers, Inc.
2627 Caves Road
Owings Mills, Maryland 21117

Published simultaneously in Canada by Houghton Mifflin Company Ltd., Markham, Ontario

A Barbara Holdridge book
Printed and bound in the United States of America

First Edition

Library of Congress Cataloging in Publication Data
Stricker, William F., 1903-1976.
  Keeping Christmas.

  "A Barbara Holdridge book."
  1. Christmas—Maryland—Baltimore. 2. Christmas
—United States. 3. Baltimore (Md.)—Social life
and customs. I. Title.
GT4986.M35S8 1981   394.2'68282'0973   81-9406
ISBN 0-916144-60-7   AACR2

Contents

The publishers express appreciation to the author's niece, Constance Harris, for encouraging the publication of this unique manuscript, for lending precious memorabilia—including the original model railroad cars described herein —so that the artist could depict them faithfully, and for her unfailing enthusiasm, cooperation and guidance in assuring that this book would remain true to the spirit of her late uncle's early life and remembrances.

KEEPING CHRISTMAS

BUT ONCE A YEAR

1 But Once a Year

WHEN I FIRST became aware of Christmas, I associated it with the fragrance of a cedar tree. Late on Christmas Eve, my childhood home in Baltimore filled with its scent. My parents, being frugal, delayed the selection of a tree until the vendors were ready to give their last one away or even pay, perhaps, to have it carted off. True, the best trees would be gone, but a perfect specimen was not necessary in our household.

My parents could adapt any tree to suit our needs. Usually the tree was too tall and had to be forced into the room which mother had chosen for the celebration. Rather than sawing off branches, father preferred to let the top of the tree bend across the ceiling. He placed the tree's base into a holder, bolted the holder to the floor, looped two strands of wire halfway up the tree trunk and pulled the wire through an iron hook in the wall. The wire was tightened, and the tree was pressed against the wall.

Next came the decorations. Balls of red, blue and an occasional silver or gold were hung by the dozens. The colors were so bright and rich that I have gone through life convinced

that their particular shades were the truest. These six-inch spheres reflected everything in the room and cast spectrums on the ceiling. If the tree became full before all ornaments were hung, extra balls were attached to wire and suspended from the ceiling.

In addition to Christmas balls, the tree groaned under the weight of tiny musical tops, stags in flight, fairies with gossamer wings, peacocks and tropical fish. Large bunches of tin grapes, painted in their natural reds, blues and greens, looked as right on our tree as on a vine. Red hearts throbbed and competed with stars, crowns, angels, Venetian lanterns and spears. From the top of the tree to the lowest limb, a chain of small colored balls was draped from branch to branch.

The tree's shine and glint mellowed under candlelight, and even as a tot I was allowed to stay up long enough to watch father fix the tree's candles. First, father carefully arranged about two dozen candles on the tree. He placed them so that no part of the tree was in darkness and no limb was in danger of being ignited. As soon as the last wick caught fire, the house lights were dimmed. The flaming tree stood out in the darkness — the most beautiful sight in the world! The candles burned themselves out in about half an hour; then off to bed for me, my brothers and my sisters.

When dawn arrived on Christmas morning, we were quickly roused and dressed for church. I simply cannot remember a childhood Christmas without snow, and vividly recall the early morning trudge through the snow to church. As I entered the doorway, a bright sign high on the apse met my eyes and proclaimed "Glory to God in the Highest." To me, the glowing sign was magical and transported me to another world. I breathed quietly. If I had to sniffle, I sniffled quietly. All of us rambunctious children listened silently to a story, old and lovely, about an infant in the manger. We were reverent without knowing its definition.

Anxious as we were to get back to the toyland at home, we paused after the service to gaze at the life-size nativity scene inside the church. Mary and Joseph, shepherds and kings, a mule, a cow and several sheep gazed down at baby Jesus and looked solemn in the dim light of two ancient reflectors.

Outside the church, grown folk wished each other "Merry Christmas," while youngsters began to boast of the gifts waiting for them at home. My parents did not give us the opportunity to compare expectations or to discuss the ingenuity of Santa Claus. We were quickly taken into custody for the walk home.

Before the advent of the automobile, the streets on a snowy Christmas morning were quiet beyond belief. The street cleaners had the day off, so all new snow remained. If the snowfall was heavy, not even the sound of a horse could be heard. No one liked to drive or ride a horse through snow, and in those days, horses had friends who remonstrated with owners daring to work a horse on Christmas Day. Apart from the sound of snow crunching under foot and shouts of "Merry Christmas," the silence was pierced only by the muffled strains of horns and drums being played indoors. Christmas, like the snow, was everywhere.

On our return from church, we entered at the back door to prevent our collision with secret Christmas preparations at the front of the house. From this rear entrance, we could hear our nearby colored brethren sing, "Go tell it on the Mountain,/ That Jesus Christ is born."

The next hurdle was breakfast. Once in the house and out of coats and hats, we were told, "Come to the breakfast table" and "No presents until breakfast is eaten." What was the menu? I don't remember. My imagination was on the other side of the house in "that room."

Only after breakfast did father guide us into the dining room, where stockings too large and too white to be ours dangled from the mantelpiece. Since Santa had to use the dining room chimney for his exit, without delay and without witnesses, each child quickly took down the stocking with his or her name on it. The stockings were stuffed with French candy, apples, walnuts, butternuts, pecans, almonds, filberts, an orange or two and — at the toe — a brand-new penny. I knew that nothing had been overlooked when I reached that penny.

After my stocking was empty I was delirious with excitement, for now was the time to enter the room with the tree and the big presents. Father opened the portals to "that room" and told us to turn a sharp right inside the door. There in front of us stood Santa Claus! I was paralyzed in the too-close presence of Santa, an unknown person in a false face with a ferry-slip beard, a pair of gloves and a red blanket that covered all traces of anything human. The voice sounded like nobody I had ever heard.

My first appearance before Santa was an occasion of trepidation, if not of terror. Here was something from another world, from which even the police could not rescue me. Moreover, the way he reviewed my record and lectured me on my vices left me trembling. In panic, I promised extravagantly to reform, even to eat breakfast.

Later, when I was a mature ten years old, I began to doubt the genuineness of Santa Claus. I figured this benefactor must be a convict, for I believed every respectable citizen at Christmastime was in his own home and not masquerading. Actually Santa was played by a nephew for over a generation.

Once, during Prohibition, a vat of spiked eggnog was produced. Santa Claus, like everybody else, had been "taking cultures of eggnog." Having played Santa long enough, he skipped out, changed into street clothes and returned to join the festivities. For my benefit, my grandfather exclaimed, "Why, here's Mr. M., and he's missed Santa!" I said to my mother, "But Ma, he smells like Santa."

The Santa I encountered at home always smelled like vanilla and nutmeg. As with other things associated with Santa Claus, I asked why, and was told that Santa had come to our home straight from the "vanilla works," a factory ten miles from home.

After Santa Claus disappeared in a cloud of vanilla and nutmeg, my attention moved to the toys. And what toys — all

shiny and new without any signs of dirt, cracks or chips. Perhaps Santa thought more highly of me than I believed.

Toy dishes, wardrobes, dresses and dolls went to my sisters, while the boys received carpenter's tools, wagons, drums and the annual Christmas horn. (Invariably, the horn was blown out of commission before "taps" on Christmas Day.) Under the tree one year was a fire engine of the old steamer type with hook and ladder. The tillerman squatted under the aerial ladder, and three galloping stallions pulled the apparatus. Every piece was made from heavy cast-iron. Another well-loved gift was an open patrol wagon for transporting criminals in warm weather. With every turn of the wagon's wheels, a tiny policeman clubbed a tinier clown.

Articles of clothing were received with less enthusiasm. Even masquerade costumes were not in demand, for we boys believed that a disguise was unmanly. In Union Square, where I lived in Baltimore, merchants did not even stock the special outfits for cowboys and Indians. Our closeness to the stockyard and familiarity with the cattle drovers made cowpunching appear far from glamorous. Since Indians were expected to lose all wars and be taken, none too gently, into captivity, no one wanted to play the role of Indian.

Each Christmas my electric toy train and tracks were brought out of storage and operated for the season. Its return was like a new gift, even though I had to fight male adults for the chance to run it. Since the first house I lived in was not wired for electricity, my train ran on current supplied by batteries. To shorten the visits of those inclined to spend excessive time playing with my train, father made guests bring their own batteries. After we moved to a house with electricity, father still delayed putting the train on the house current, in order to prevent miniature buffs from running up the electric bill. Years later the train was finally modified to run from a transformer.

A few of my childhood friends had mechanical train sets. These trains ran on tracks, but were not electrically powered.

The train contained a main spring, and as the spring unwound, the train ran on the tracks. The drawback of this variety was that the wheels of the locomotive had to be held until the engine was coupled with the track. Preceding both the mechanical and the electric train was the steam-powered toy train, which had actual steam boilers. The steam was jetted into tiny cylinders to work the pistons and main shafts, just as on a life-size iron horse.

At the same time my train set came out of hiding, my sisters' best dolls were returned to them. Each of my sisters had a large doll with a bisque or Dresden china head, wigs of human hair and eyes that opened and closed. One doll even moaned "Mama" when squeezed. These dolls, like my trains, were never intended for everyday use; the dolls appeared only at Christmas and Easter. Such was the care lavished on them that today they are still being mothered by the granddaughters and greatgranddaughters of the original owners.

Most toys under the tree were meant to be played with and enjoyed for good, which was not for long. Almost every boy received a drum to thump and beat into junk before sundown. I can recall only one exception, a drum that had been carried through the Civil War. Both its owner and myself could sit on the drum without injuring it, so we judged that the assaults it sustained by way of percussions were equal or heavier than our combined weights.

Santa did not turn out tools that stood up under the manly vigor of his clients. The carpenter's tools I received came to grief in my first attempt to use them in turning packing cases into a clubhouse on some vacant lot. When I proudly showed the hammer out of such a tool kit to a veteran cabinetmaker, he smiled and said, "It's a very nice hammer, but don't hit anything with it!"

Popguns were not so easy to destroy, but they were apt to be confiscated under your nose or to disappear mysteriously. The toy market of today presents many perfect facsimiles, except in weight, of lethal guns, from the frontier "Peacemaker" down to the snub-nosed, one-inch barrel revolver. Seventy years ago, air rifles and knives were excusable gifts for farm boys who might have use for them, but they were thought too dangerous for city lads. In that honest age, a boy aspired to be on the right side of the law. Being a gangster had no appeal. Any boy who took the part of the bandit in street games did so because he was chosen by lot, or else had to take his turn when the roles rotated, or was not well liked.

When I was too old for popguns, a game of checkers was included in my annual haul. My parents felt checkers made a scholarly appearance under the tree. We children did not play the game with wisdom but with spirit; this recreation caused such arguments that the set was often burned by the authorities before New Year's Day.

On Christmas morning, we quite freely pulled out and inspected all toys. Unless intended for someone outside the family, the gifts were never wrapped. My parents watched us play until they were sure no further instruction was needed on the operation or assembly of some new gadget. Happily knowing our interest was going to be held for some time, mother and father withdrew from the room, pleased with the success of their Christmas preparations.

MR. WILLIE AND MISS KATIE

2 Mr. Willie and Miss Katie

MY PARENTS WERE KNOWN to each other and respectfully throughout the whole neighborhood as Mr. Willie and Miss Katie. I cannot remember them without grey hair, but also I cannot remember when they were not physically strong.

Mr. Willie's paternal forebears had been in America before the Revolution, and his great-grandfather had distinguished himself in the War of 1812. His mother came from Ireland before the Civil War and was reputed to have the most enviable berth of anybody in domestic service in Baltimore. One of her contemporaries observed that "her job was so good the back of her dress was worn out from sitting down!"

Father's first job was the trade of a bookbinder, but he was soon discovered by the politicians and became an employee of the federal government at the age of twenty-three. After seventeen years of commuting seventy-five miles a day to that job, he resigned in favor of a job in Baltimore. He became the city's most responsible bookkeeper and held this job for some thirty years. At the age of seventy-two, he retired. For recreation, Mr. Willie sang bass in a male quartet. Every Christmas the group sang carols for the inmates of the Baltimore jail and always ended their concert for the men behind bars with "God Rest Ye Merry, Gentlemen."

Miss Katie claimed German extraction: her mother, an uncle and two aunts immigrated from Baden. On her father's side, her ancestry was not clear. Her father's recital alternated between the Celts when sober and the American Indians when otherwise. Miss Katie was the second oldest daughter in a family of thirteen children.

Mother's idea of a good time was a card game or a fancy funeral. Her knowledge of funerals was so complete that more than one funeral director consulted Miss Katie for advice on deportment at wakes and gravesides. Since she classified people according to who was respectable enough for this mortician or who would have to make do with another, funeral directors asked her to recommend families likely to favor them with business.

At the time of her death, Miss Katie had been married forty years. Mr. Willie survived her by eight years.

Mr. Willie's occupation at City Hall influenced the gifts that came to our house at Christmas. Since he devoted his leisure to advising ward executives in Italian, German and Yiddish, his support was sought by all who had ambitions for a municipal job, including charwomen, lamplighters, jail guards and morgue attendants. He was always doing favors for somebody at City Hall, which amounted to being a high-class errand boy. Favorably regarded by tradesmen, mechanics and taxpayers in our neighborhood, Mr. Willie carried their tax money, usually in currency, down to the office in the morning and returned with their receipts at night. The commission merchants along the wharves, the farmers in the markets, and even a pawnshop operator knew my father.

Mr. Willie's acquaintances flooded our house with gifts. In came peanuts and vegetables by the bushels, grapes by the crate, and apples by the box. In came dressed poultry and homemade sausage from the farmers whose market licenses had expired and needed yearly adjustment. Sweet cider arrived in wholesale lots and was most welcome to both children and adults. Wine was offered but returned; Miss Katie made wine from anything that would ferment, including dandelions and parsnips.

A question of great delicacy arose over some cigars, which came from a character claiming to be the "Champion Cigar Dispenser of the State." Mr. Willie had the impression that all contestants for this championship should be required to dispense the "seegars" singly. Since this champion distributed his cigars by the box, Mr. Willie thought the contest unfair and refused the gift. The quality of these cigars was felonious, and no one missed them anyway.

Oysters arrived by the barrel. One batch was taken to a small unheated room on the second floor back, which served as a cold storage space. Family friends usually gathered in the second floor front and helped themselves to oysters on their way down the backstairs to the kitchen. A dentist and a frequenter of our house had a phenomenal appetite for oysters. On a two-week trip from Baltimore, he carried oysters with him instead of clothing.

Noting the high quality of the oysters we had been given one year, the dentist and a few cronies came to feast in our back room. The dentist had free run of the house, so no one bothered to check on his oyster-tasting. By morning, the dentist and accomplices had the room knee-deep in shells. Miss Katie delivered a fierce ultimatum to the dentist, who devoted a morning to carting oyster shells to the garbage.

From then on, all oysters were relegated to a two-story brick house that stood in our backyard. Mr. Willie and friends sloshed the oysters with a mixture of salt, cornmeal and water; this diet was believed to be necessary for fat and contented oysters. Whether it was I cannot swear, although I listened to noises described to me as being the happy slurping of oysters.

One of the most appreciated gifts of my childhood was a simple, indestructible wooden boat. Hewn by hand out of the discarded end of a two-by-four, the boat was a labor of love from an odd-job man, who washed our front steps and kept the pavement free of leaves. In return, he received his usual Christmas gift of a piece of money and a mysterious something else. Mr. Willie also gave him free counsel on how to make the most of his money.

Another person who gave the intangible gift of his originality was Jake. A harmless creature and a bachelor, he could be trusted with anything of no value. Jake was a street sweeper and artfully managed to entice daily lunches from the housewives along the wake of his broom and his sorcery. His promiscuous cadging of the season's more exquisite victuals was offset by his generosity to children. Parents could not begrudge him fine food when he gave such wonderful gifts to their heirs. Besides, how could the parents know those beautiful goldfish came from the pond in the city square?

Jake gave to Christmas in another manner, a gift not well appreciated by the community. He had noted that street singers were lavish with carols before Christmas Day, but lost interest on the actual day; he decided to remedy this lack by going into recital alone, with a voice of evident imperfections and loud volume. In the wee hours, his rendition of "Silent Night" roused the police watch, who brought him into the station.

One understanding judge regarded Jake not as a problem of the judiciary but as an artist trying to improve his technique. This magistrate dismissed the hour of the recital as irrelevant and immaterial and decided Jake was the victim of callous cads. Without fail, the sympathetic judge would take Jake straight from the cage to lunch.

One gift came to our household as a tribute to the talents of Kate, our laundress. The gift was an eighth of a barrel of Pilsner from Gus's, the corner tavern, in appreciation of the size of the monthly settlements made there for the treatment of our washerwoman's thirst. In those days, the average woman who went out to work was expected to operate at her best and be happy on "a pint of dark a day." Our Amazon was far superior to others who sweated over the tubs. She carried her load well, but had greater needs to supply. Her fluid replacement ran to a heroic amount, and Gus was gratified to receive a person of her grand intake and respectable mien. Kate was never judged guilty of that indelicate indecorum of showing her liquor.

At Christmas our laundress Kate began to put on airs. She claimed her doctor told her not to eat dark meat of fowl, or shin, or stew meats, or forequarters beef, or spareribs. Her diet required white meat, round steak, or pork off the rib or neck. When she broke the news, Miss Katie thought her allowance at the corner saloon must be overdrawn.

Close enough to the holiday for Miss Katie to blame her demise on "too rich food," Kate sickened and died. Her distraught husband was in no condition to make decisions, so Miss Katie took over the funeral plans. As neighbors had spread the unfounded rumor that her own prize washerwoman had departed this life by hanging herself, Miss Katie had the corpse dressed in a good nightgown with a needlepoint lace ruffle around the neck. Miss Katie also stipulated that the casket be opened all the way down to show off the pair of fancy silk hose that she donated and itched to be rid of.

When our washerwoman's remains were exhibited in our front room, the widower thought the display most gorgeous and found great consolation in the thought that no more lovely funeral ever issued from the byway in which he dwelt. Years later he often mentioned the funeral, and when his descriptive powers had reached their limit, he would sum it up in the simple sentence, "It was just like a Christmas tree."

Although Mr. Willie and Miss Katie gave, and gave mostly

to those unable to make any sort of return, I cannot remember their giving gifts to each other. During childhood, I was so engrossed by the first sight of my gifts on Christmas Day that their exchange could have escaped my notice. After childhood, I am sure it did not happen.

Almost all the gifts they received were perishable, and, with the exception of the spirits and tobacco, were consumed by the entire household. One of the few lasting articles Miss Katie received was a weatherproof wreath on a small wire easel; this item served as a lifetime flower service for many funerals, with my mother's compliments. For himself, Mr. Willie cherished an ornate toothpick carved from the bone handle of a toothbrush and made for him by a prison inmate.

Obviously Mr. Willie and Miss Katie kept their basic wants down. They allowed themselves few luxuries and were most unselfish. They seldom bought new clothes, but bought good things made to order. While shopping, they could be deterred by a price tag. When they learned the price of something they liked but could not afford, they always remarked, "Well, we still have each other." At Christmas, I suspect, they spent all they had on family and friends.

The gifts my parents offered were not sumptuous, ornate or overrefined, but all were sure to give pleasure. Receiving them brought me a warmth of heart then and a warmth of recollection now, a warmth never to be more than inadequately expressed.

SHOULD AULD ACQUAINTANCE

3 Should Auld Acquaintance

AMONG MR. WILLIE's acquaintances were dignitaries of varying shades of importance. Father's occupation required him to meet with the governor infrequently, with the mayor monthly, with different ward executives and inspectors irregularly and with the taxpayers daily. He was on the best of terms with police captains, reporters, criminal lawyers, the wardens of three penal institutions, a superintendent of Baltimore's asylum, a custodian of the morgue, and a hangman.

But our guest list was limited to those of less sensational calling. Family friends came all the year round and were taken for granted by the household, although their antics were thought quite flamboyant by those who rarely encountered them.

Most of Miss Katie's friends were kept at home by

housekeeping duties, but three did appear regularly. One was the wife of a huckster and a total abstainer. Another was a widow and served as first maid to a wealthy lady, whose airs she imitated while drinking whisky. The third and most frequent female visitor was married to Charley, one of Mr. Willie's closest friends. Her name was Alice, and she was devoted to works of religion and martinis.

Poor Alice began ailing, and her doctor forbade her to drink alcohol. For all of twenty-four hours Alice abstained; then she decided to return to having a cocktail or two without Charley's knowledge. For his own part, Charley had decided to spare Alice's feelings by never drinking in front of her. At a Christmas dinner one year, Alice arrived early with the intention of sneaking a few before Charley's entrance. To fool him, she filled a teapot with martinis and drank from a dainty china cup. When Charley arrived, he was furnished with a teapot of manhattans. They both proceeded to acquire a lovely glow and never said a word about their teas.

In addition to Charley, who was a retired train conductor, father's social roster included Jim, an ex-policeman; Sam, a retired postman; and Jack, a policeman on active duty. A peculiar frame of mind obsessed these characters and the others mentioned in this memoir. They pitied the poor and with a bit of inducement could wax maudlin about poverty. Yet if the Almighty created any poorer than they, He must have kept them in hiding. I took them for very important people, who were very kind to me. At this distance of years, they still seem stout souls, who made this world enchanting without ever contributing to its wealth, its progress or its genius.

When I was old enough to roam the streets, I became friendly with the policemen I knew, especially my father's friend Jack. Jack had been coming to the house as long as I could remember, and on Sunday afternoons, Jack and Mr. Willie would take me for a walk. The two of them usually went into places filled with cigar smoke and cardplayers, and I would be stuck in a corner with a ham and Swiss cheese sandwich. As a sandwich came with every place we went, I always had a bag full by the time I got home.

Jack was about the same size as Mr. Willie; both being just short of six feet. Jack had a turned-up nose, a protruding underlip, and small eyes in a chubby face, which shrank under his large helmet. Although he was a very effective policeman, he never rose above the rank of private. "His penmanship wasn't too good," and he often asked Mr. Willie to read something for him because "he had forgotten his glasses." My father liked him, because he was above corruption and paid for what he drank. (Mr. Willie either forgot or overlooked the many times when he paid for Jack's booze.)

A mild-spoken man and, I believe, a compassionate one, Jack seemed to his superiors capable of handling problems of any magnitude. As a result, he was moved all over the city to quell the more notable breaches of peace, including tumults in the slums, stevedores' strikes and rioting sailors. His treatment was sudden and anesthetic when a "bad man" had to be faced, and subdued when not.

On one occasion an enormous murderer was loose in Jack's district. Learning the criminal's location, Jack spotted the four-hundred-pound suspect asleep in a rocker. The man had his shoes off and a howitzer on the hassock beside him. Jack went to a blacksmith, who bent and flattened a yard loop of one-inch steel cable, and returned to his quarry. He shed his shoes and coat and crept within striking distance for a brief and businesslike encounter.

A few minutes later, Jack carried out the howitzer, put on his coat and shoes, and notified the precinct of the need for a wagon "for a stretcher case." When the wagon and more police arrived, they found the unconscious felon's left wrist manacled to his left ankle.

Only once was Jack known to have shot at a man. He and his partner were fired upon by thugs whom they surprised ransacking a warehouse. A gun battle ensued, and Jack's partner was killed. Never again, except for target practice or a rare flourish to edify the recalcitrant on a new post, did Jack resort to firearms.

Jack's appearance in our kitchen was always welcome. He would show up before going on night duty and claim that his wife had gone out to do some church work. This remark meant he was hungry. To make sure he was properly nourished, Miss Katie would serve him his favorite, ham and steamed slaw, and to this, Mr. Willie added a growler of beer. Although Jack said he did not care for sweets, he would turn off a twelve-inch pie in a casual manner.

Jack loved to play with my toys. On the pretext of explaining their operation, he would get down on the floor with me. He took special pleasure in my cast-iron patrol wagon, and as he ran it back and forth across the floor, he would talk about his experiences with the life-size model. That wagon vanished from my toy box, and mother explained that Santa needed it back. I always wondered about its disappearance until years later when I got a surprised glimpse of it. The table centerpiece at a dinner honoring Jack's retirement from the police force was my very own patrol wagon.

When I met this next policeman, he had already retired from duty. A tall, thin, impressive man with white hair, Jim was another close friend of the family. After rising to foreman in a hair factory, Jim branched out into politics, became a patrolman, and finally a court bailiff. He thought being court bailiff was a less versatile chore than policing, and retired. Jim had triumphed over an alcoholic trauma in his youth, but allowed himself an ounce of rye whiskey before dinner on the advice of his physician. He did everything in moderation and with much thought.

Jim never tired of telling one unusual Christmas story.

"Jack's appearance in the kitchen was always welcome...."

When he was a policeman, he had vowed never to arrest any-body on Christmas Day. Jim and the rest of the force in his district, which was, by the way, pronounced "dee-strict," had an understanding with the desk sergeant. The agreement was that the police blotter be kept clean of felonies and misdemeanors on Christmas Day. Anything resembling one was booked as of December 24 between 11:00 p.m. and midnight or as of December 26 between midnight and 1:00 a.m.

Although often provoked, Jim stuck to this determination until an unappreciated and harmless genius wanted to be taken to jail. To please this man, Jim finally charged him with the technical pretext of "attempting undue influence on an officer." Jim took his "prisoner" to the watch house and learned that the culprit had been to the station earlier that day and had practiced his skills as an electrician. (This career was not widely pursued at the turn of the century.) Yearning to have his art and mystery brought to public attention, the prisoner-electrician had created a sample of his ability. Over the squire's rostrum (magistrates were referred to as squires in those days) glared a wreath of red and green lightbulbs. The wreath surrounded the legend "6.45," which was a favorite phrase of the bench. It referred to the usual fine for misdemeanors — five dollars plus costs or $6.45. "That electrician really put the Christmas spirit into the judiciary system," Jim would say.

Another almost constant companion of Mr. Willie was Charley. Some years before father's retirement, Charley had left a long career with the railroad. Charley was a quiet man of great refinement and very little schooling. Born and bred in the mountains, he was dedicated to the study of railroad schedules and trout streams. His father had been a railroader and had died in a train wreck. Charley followed his father's life work and took to railroading as soon as he was of age. Because of his quiet refinement, Charley was quickly promoted to conductor on the best, extra-fare luxury train in operation. Charley lived up to the stateliness of the job by being very attentive to every word spoken, by bowing from the waist, and by making his passengers feel important.

Charley wore spectacles and a heavy moustache, which turned up slightly at the corner ends due to his habit of giving it one brush upward with the back of his index finger. Usually he did this to keep his moustache out of his beer, and any ladies present watched for this chic gesture and tittered.

But Charley's career received a serious setback, and he was forced into an early retirement. Once, when his train started twenty minutes late, Charley set the schedule for maximum speed. To bolster their skills around the curves, Charley and the engineer drank a horn or two of whiskey. Unfortunately for them, their picture was snapped while they were drinking. The train arrived on time, but its conductor and engineer were put out of work.

Because of his railroad background, Charley laid out the tracks for my toy train. No roadbed ever was treated to more conscientious surveying. Just as the outside rail had to be raised on the curves of the main iron on a real railroad, Charley raised it on my set in the parlor. When the train set was disassembled after Christmas, I discovered his secret — beer bottle caps were placed under the outside end of the cross ties at every curve.

About this same time, my parents began experimenting with mixed drinks. Mr. Willie and Miss Katie were advised to have one before the evening meal, but they disliked the taste of straight liquor. A variety of cocktails was tried until they and their friends began to develop a taste for these concoctions. The manhattan became the most popular drink, so Miss Katie decided it would be nice to have plenty on hand for Christmas. The manhattan, she was told, got better with age, and should be mixed and let to cure. At the end of October, Miss Katie prepared about five gallons worth and put the beverage down in the basement to age.

When manhattans came into our family's life, so did Sam.

Sam was an ex-postman and the image of Theodore Roosevelt. Always curious to know how the manhattans were doing, Sam limited his visits to the last quarter of the year. Sam would always suggest a taste test on the batch, so Charley or Mr. Willie would get a pitcher, go to the cellar, and return with a taste (four rounds apiece) for the three men. Sam was handicapped in his drinking; he had the "shakes" and had difficulty steadying the glass against his lips. But if somebody had the kindness to hold the glass for him, his drinking ability was prodigious.

Given the opportunity, Sam would have drunk five gallons of manhattans in one sitting. To prevent this, Mr. Willie and Charley discovered a way to speed Sam's exit. He was highly vulnerable to the song "When You and I Were Young, Maggie." Upon hearing this tune, Sam would weep and grieve and head home, so Mr. Willie kept the phonograph loaded and ready to discharge. Whenever Sam had had enough, on would go "When You and I Were Young, Maggie" and out would go Sam in tears.

The ultimate earthly decline of Sam was one of splendor. Since his youth, he had been the dedicated and active member of a fraternal lodge. The lodge was so secretive that even its members were in ignorance of its purpose. Their regalia was like nothing on earth. As Sam advanced through the various dignities of the order, his get-up became more ornate and his titles more illustrious and exalted. I could never keep abreast of Sam's titles, so my father simplified the whole plan of advancement by telling me that Sam was on his way to becoming the "Great High Wang." Sam loved the splendor and dazzled us every time his costume was embellished or changed to another. Next to the Christmas tree, he was the most brilliant thing ever seen in our house.

When Sam departed this life he hoped to go in all the glories of the lodge. On his deathbed he had to be reassured constantly until Mr. Willie hit upon a scheme that gave Sam complete comfort. When my father was assured that Sam was dying, he and Jack dressed Sam in his full regalia from ceremonial hat to fancy boots and held up a mirror at the foot of the bed, to give Sam an idea of how he would appear when laid out. Sam died relieved and happy.

Jack and Mr. Willie never found a person who admitted to being a lodge brother of Sam's, and no one in fancy dress attended the funeral. Sam, they suspected, belonged to a lodge of his own founding and solitary membership.

TO ENTERTAIN STRANGERS

4 To Entertain Strangers

MY FAMILY SELDOM went abroad for amusement, because much better entertainment came to us at home. Many of our visitors explained their escapades and woes to Miss Katie or Mr. Willie, and I learned much just by watching and listening. In my later years, I saw eminent professional entertainers who were no improvement over the tragedies and comedies that passed through the doors of my childhood.

Certain fictional characters are said to be great characters, precisely because they are great fools. The environment of my young days included very few who were devoid of all powers of understanding or who frittered away their time and talent to no purpose. Instead, my neighborhood was filled with the serious simpleton, the individual who plied an almost futile means of earning a living but the best or only means within his competence.

One such Christmas visitor was Frank. At his christening, he had received a much fancier name, too fancy to be used in his level of culture. Frank was innocent of all malice, had handicaps of speech and mind, and was the only child and sole support of his widowed mother, whose gifts as a shrew all respected. Frank worked for a factory.

Facetiously known as the "college," the factory was named by immigrants studying English, and by natives who had not made it to the third grade. This plant processed hogs' hair, which was used to make upholstery for carriages and hacks. Early in the morning the hair was laid out on the bare ground to dry. By noon it was dry enough to be recovered, and Frank's job six days a week from noon to dark was to do just that—gather up the dry hair by hand.

On the Sabbath, Frank's only free day of the week, he gave his time and limited talents to minding babies gratis, holding the doctor's horse, and running volunteer interference for policemen in pursuit of criminals or lunatics. Frank also spent Sunday going to church and having heart-to-heart talks with alley urchins, whose kites he mended and pets he doctored. Too poor even to own an overcoat, Frank's travels were limited in the winter months. He was only able to visit us at Christmas when someone loaned him a warm coat.

Back in the days when automobiles were novel monsters, Frank became a hero for an afternoon. An automobile caught fire and was quickly abandoned by its passengers. While neighbors cowered in trees, under cellar doors and behind fences, Frank walked right up to the car, tore open the hood, exhaled like a tornado, and blew the fire out. His heroism was rewarded by a collection, mostly in copper, from a grateful public. The money, though, could not compare with his first taste of glory,

Frank and the Auto

and the glory could not compare with a good full plate of Miss Katie's pastry and a quart or two of cold cider. Not knowing when Frank would be able to escape his mother and visit us again, my parents filled Frank with food and drink while they had him.

One Sunday afternoon, Mr. Willie learned that Frank's latest dinner had consisted of "lots of cups of coffee and lots of pieces of bread and butter." Questioning revealed that "lots" was two, and "butter" was lard sprinkled with coarse salt, a spread immigrants favored as the most economical silencer of voracious children. No high-calorie man like Mr. Willie could associate such repast with his idea of dinner.

Immediately, with Frank in tow, Mr. Willie visited a private abattoir for steaks, a bakery for hot rolls with genuine butter, and a nearby brewery for beverage. The brewery's fireman who had often served as emergency chef for my father broiled the steaks in the furnace and poured beer from the keg always on tap and at the disposal of the employees. Then and there Frank entered a new world of wonders, for Frank had reached maturity without knowing such food existed.

This new world soon came down on Frank's ears. Mr. Willie delivered Frank to his home and ran afoul of his mother. She excoriated them both for being debauched by the capitalists, denounced Mr. Willie as an agent of Satan, and called Creation to witness that Mr. Willie had come to bring anarchy to her house and perdition to her offspring. Father made a speedy exit, and Frank was left standing at the doorway like a lonesome and stupified clown—a clown with red hair, enormous ears and a flat head.

Another character who absorbed what he could of our hospitality was George. When George turned up at our house, he was a grinder of scissors and cutlery. He was a man of abilities, many and clever, despite his low occupation. George traveled with a portable grindstone, which was the only thing that stood between him and a vagrancy charge. He had seen better days, with two eyes, but now had only one; poor George had to sleep with that one eye open due to the kind of wives he married.

Among other legends that grew up around George was that he had played the vaudeville circuit with a musical goat. He got the goat's cooperation in a "Mammy" song by prodding the goat at the right moment with a sharpened finishing nail. After living on the same diet relished by George, the goat died. George's sorrow at this loss was mitigated by the fact that the goat had been a liability in his wooing of women.

Usually George showed up at our house the day after Christmas with a hankering to eat filberts and to drink what he called "that there sweet muscatelle," a wine Miss Katie made from a combination of fruit juices, rinds, resins, and sugar. A pound of filberts was laid in against his coming, and he always invited us to slake his passion for "any of them there nuts." After consuming wine and filberts, George liked to eat hard-boiled eggs and a dill pickle and to toast the family. With many cheers, he invoked the hope that we would be long attended by the prosperity which supplied these delicacies. Miss Katie picked up any scraps for his own Christmas board back in "shirttail row," a place of residence not dignified enough for the word alley, and George was on his way.

At Christmas we also entertained Doc. Since Doc was intrigued with human weakness, he came in the hope that our indiscretions would entertain him. He was a medical doctor, a large stout man with the gray beard grown by every man of substance from the administrations of Grant to Garfield. In fact, he had devoted his last year of medical school to the cultivation of a beard. (A well-trimmed beard bolstered the confidence of the patients.) In his own words, Doc had "brought many in and seen many out."

Doc considered poetry a disease and boasted he could have cured Milton himself. Any young sophisticate who contradicted his elders or was willing to wager his betters were wrong was believed by Doc to be suffering from poetry or prophecy, another dread disease in Doc's opinion. Prophecy was bad for public health and had to be prevented from reaching epidemic proportions. Doc, therefore, undertook to exterminate poetry and prophecy by jumping on their symptoms with both clinical feet.

In those days, Doc made his calls by horse and buggy with an agreeably silent man he called his groom. For Doc, this man was the perfect groom; he listened but never talked back. As he had been rescued from imminent death at the very start of Doc's practice, the groom also served as concrete proof of the good doctor's medical skills. At the end of the day when Doc had talked himself and his groom into fatigue, they relied on the horse to drive them home. Between the human eye and the setting sun, the contour of Doc's rig looked like a monster with arms akimbo; the nodding heads of Doc and the groom formed the elbows of the monster's silhouette.

Until the day after Christmas, Doc, the groom and the horse wore sprigs of holly as a token of their temporary truce with the world. Come December 26, the holly was removed, and Doc resumed his hunt for advanced cases of poetry and prophecy, particularly among the young. On this same day, Doc would drop by our house to "point up" his stomach with a bit of Miss Katie's country sausage and sauerkraut and to gather news.

Apparently a turkey dinner left Doc with the sense that not all the holes and corners of his stomach had been properly visited. To remedy this gastric condition and to disinfect the intestines, Doc prescribed country sausage and sauerkraut. Miss Katie's sausage and sauerkraut, he believed, were flawless. Mother cooked her sauerkraut the day before serving it and then simmered it with a net bag of fresh onion and shredded crab-apples or green apples. The sausage was carefully stuffed by her own hands.

Often Doc entranced us children with stories of feats he had performed as a surgeon. He had cured a parrot of scratching its ears and had grown a beak on a canary to enable it to defend itself against the parrot. He had operated on a dog, so it could climb trees, while a cat was transformed to a barking dog. One of

his ambitions was to endow a dog with the gift of speech. Once he produced a skull from a lady's hatbox and told us children, "I cleaned this fellow up this morning before breakfast." The victim, we were told mournfully, died of "candy poisoning." With a tear in his voice, doc said, "I pity you young addicts."

Doc himself had symptoms—those of philanthropy. He often set off on missions to rescue the poor and the starving, but these missions seemed to go awry. One Christmas Eve, a very embarrassed Doc and groom rocketed from the home of a Sicilian widow and her daughters. Apparently Doc had heard that these women had been reduced to eating plain spaghetti and anchovies and were starving. Bent on heading off an epidemic of malnutrition, Doc and his man had entered the widow's house loaded with victuals. Actually these women were observing the strict fast customary in their native country for the Christmas vigil, and they forced the men to exit in demoralized ignominy.

These were blissful days when the social security of one's neighbor was the private concern of every individual. Nobody could stomach the terrifying possibility that a friend might go undernourished at Christmas. Eating was an important way to celebrate. On the other hand, in my neighborhood, Christmas cards were thought ridiculous. They weren't edible, so what was their purpose?

THE LAND OF LILLIPUT

5 The Land of Lilliput

AROUND THE FIRST of October, artisans and tradesmen began working on astounding Christmas spectacles called miniature gardens. These gardens were scale models of winter scenes, and in Union Square, the idea to make them originated at the fire hall. In the comparative tranquility of the firehouse and without proper tools and model kits, firemen devoted their leisure to making miniature houses, churches, mills, stables, trolley cars, ocean liners and, most naturally, fire equipment.

At Christmas, local firehouses competed for the best display.

Every truck and every engine company had its own fans and self-appointed publicity men. The firemen faithfully duplicated local suburbs and villages with their unmistakable landmarks, such as silos, stand pipes, railroad yards, and cemeteries. Sometimes these scenes were enlivened by special mechanical effects; the more complicated the animation the better I liked the garden. One fire company contrived a garden with a periodic fire and spurting water to put out the recurring blaze. What renewed the fire is still unknown, for the inventor perished in the line of duty and took his secret with him.

The garden's topography was formed with fine mesh wire on which plaster of paris was formed and set. The surface was painted, usually white for snow. To make the snow sparkle, powdered mica or isinglass was scattered on top, or the surface was sprinkled with beer and epsom salts. After the beer evaporated, the stranded salt crystals suggested glistening snow.

The gardens were enormous; displays from thirty to forty-five yards were not uncommon. The largest were made in sections and later assembled. In small fire halls, space was saved by slanting part of the garden up the rear wall. To make a slanted garden work required an understanding of perspective, but the firemen were ingenious. Besides, their inventiveness was encouraged by understanding chief inspectors who prided themselves on having the best displays in their district.

Simpler gardens were produced by shopkeepers for their store windows. But these public displays did not attract me as much as the special handiwork of artistic friends. These amateurs invited me and my family to contemplate the fruit of their patience and effort. While some imitated what they saw at the fire station or toy shop, many more were original productions. All were put together after business hours by craftsmen who had already put in ten or twelve hours of labor in the foundry, brewery, blacksmith shop or slaughterhouse.

In particular, I recall the clerk of a small grocery store. He constructed in miniature a solemn ceremony in a medieval cathedral. The project took twenty years of scrupulous concentration and three-fourths of his wife's parlor. The idea did not come from any of his customers, who were unlearned and untraveled, but from a colored print left him by a friend. The grocery clerk scaled every item perfectly and duplicated the picture exactly. Tiny candles were placed on ornate altars, which were complete down to the veins in the marble. Even a restless child was struck by the magnificence of the cathedral.

The community encouraged these private citizens by offering a prize of five dollars for first place, a guinea hen for second, and a bottle of whisky for third. The college of judges was composed of a justice of the peace, a sign painter, a wheelwright, a railroad conductor, an embalmer, and others thought to be of aesthetic background. Moving from house to house, the judges took copious notes on each garden and consumed all food and drink presented to them. In fact, homes with good pastry cooks and superior punch were suspected of having a definite advantage. The judges' decisions were, however, rarely disputed.

Normally the gardens in private homes were worked on in secret and unveiled no earlier than December 25, but one man allowed me to watch his masterpiece evolving. A tailor and a house painter, he was not in demand in either profession. He looked less like any other painter I met for he did not wear overalls. In my neighborhood, overalls were worn by painters, carpenters, plasterers and bricklayers as a status symbol. This man wore pants, suspenders, a winter undershirt and no shoes year round. During the months I watched him work, he created an unbelievable snow scene.

First he covered three walls including the windows with oil cloth. For the sky, he suspended a canopy of blue cloth with tiny stars from the room's ceiling. Swags of tinsel, each one overlapping the next, were draped along the edge of the sky. The scene itself was filled with a snow-covered cave in Bethlehem, a sphinx, a pond full of skaters, signposts, a train with raw cotton billowing from its smokestack, and a detachment of infantry wearing golden helmets.

In the center of all this was an artificial tree. The tree, which was set in a revolving music box, turned to the tinkling of "Silent Night" and "O Du Frohlich." Every branch bristled with a spike of finely blown glass and a Christmas ball. At intervals, enlarged snowflakes and replicas of Lohengrin's swan passed in review. For a final touch, hidden lamps cast an orange glow over everything.

Another genius hid behind a face like a turtle. He was a sturdy character of medium height and had to fold his hands on his paunch before he was able to talk. By occupation, he was a cloth inspector for a sweatshop, and by hobby, manager of a basketball team. When "garden fever" hit him, he would wave his hands and proclaim, "This garden I'm working on has got me all, all confused."

After working all night on his Christmas garden, he became oblivious to the outside world. He would tie a four-in-hand tie delicately and precisely on a collar that wasn't there. He would board a streetcar at one intersection and get off at the next and forget why he walked into a bar. What was most unusual was that he did not have his own home in which to build his garden. He boarded with a couple who saw possibilities in their tenant's foggy state. Since he was so absent-minded, he paid his board on demand, and "on demand" meant more often than due.

His garden was remarkable; a tree was suspended from the ceiling by the top of its trunk and was revolved automatically. Grafted to the top of the tree trunk was a metal rod, which pierced the ceiling to the room above. The rod became the axle of a wheel in the floor of the room above and the axle of a wheel between the top of the tree and the ceiling. This second wheel had windmill blades with a horizontal ring of gas jets fixed below the blades. When the gas jets were lit, the pressure of their flame pushed a wheel of blades, which turned the tree. The gas jets were difficult to extinguish and to relight, so they were

The Christmas Garden

usually lit at dusk and burned for hours. Since the tree was not artificial, not fireproof, and stayed up long enough to become very likely tinder, I am surprised that the tree never caught fire. The tree seemed miraculously protected, and no one even dared to suggest the possibility of fire to the garden's creator.

This same designer was not satisfied to decorate his tree with birds, swings, or even flying fish; he had to have angels. Usually these angels flew in the same direction the tree revolved, but sometimes a misbehaving angel would do an about-face and fly stern forward. Because the tree could not be stopped easily, the wrong-way angel would have to wait until the gas jets were turned off and the exhibit closed to the public.

Thanks to the thoroughness of the scenery, a spectator could not tramp freely about the tree. The tree was surrounded by a model railroad of extraordinary realism and size. One extensive loop of track skirted the whole platform on which the garden rested, and a smaller loop crossed the platform diagonally and carried the trains into or alongside the tunnels. The tracks and crossties were made by hand, and the space between the crossties was filled with hominy to represent limestone ballast. Along either side of the right of way, poles carried telephone lines made from picture wire. No detail was forgotten.

My family's first gardens were humble affairs, but they were our best efforts. We preferred to depict summer scenes and specialized in beautiful lawns made from sawdust, which I dyed green and called moss. The lawn was intersected by straight white paths made from table salt. For variety, one year my father laid out a small replica of a professional baseball diamond and used models of the World Series teams from the past fall on the field. That year the boys of the neighborhood pronounced my family's display as one of the wonders of the season.

Miniature gardens provided some of the best entertainment of the season and they still fill an important place in my memory of Christmas. The creators of these tiny perfect worlds had no truck with mediocrity and never accepted an excuse for failure.

GETTING READY

6 Getting Ready

PREPARATIONS HAD JUST as much to do with making Christmas worth remembering as did the capers of visitors, neighbors, and local purveyors of comfort and joy. In my most Germanic neighborhood, all manner of minute preparation was undertaken to insure a proper celebration. The nobility and gentry of Baltimore imported creature comforts from St. Louis, Milwaukee, and even Munich. At Christmas, our local products were not good enough, and no one offered them to anyone but strange policemen, truant officers, dogcatchers, and other traditional enemies of man and beast.

About the middle of December, the gondola cars of the

71

railroad wandered away to the mountainous parts of the route. Days later, laden with evergreen and holly, the cars reappeared on inbound local freights. On the other side of town, young gentlemen home from boarding school prepared for Christmas and found in it cozy sophistication by reading Dickens and inhaling unaccustomed cigars. An eccentric dowager prepared for Christmas by mobilizing her friends to dress in their formal best and to serve Christmas dinner to dray horses.

Another sure sign of the approach of Christmas was the appearance of holly everywhere. Florists added holly to their stock; a shop without it might just as well hang a crepe. Holly became visible on the door of the blacksmith's shop, on the ends of the light brackets in the butcher's window, and from the tassel on the blind in the embalmer's workshop. In sprigs, it stuck out of the horse collars in the harness-maker's showcase. The display windows of the Chinamen who monopolized the laundry industry of that era were decorated with snow-white shirts and holly. Holly graced the corners of the large mirrors behind bars, while the mirrors themselves were visions of winter scenery done in soap.

To a child, the sight of holly meant it was time to start dreaming in earnest about Santa Claus. An editorial in the *New York Sun* on September 21, 1897 confirmed the existence of Santa Claus beyond all mentionable doubt. In my neighborhood, that editorial was not needed, for there were no practical skeptics. Adults asked each other, "What is Santa Claus going to bring you?" and "How did Santa Claus treat you?" These conversations convinced an eavesdropping child like myself better than any editorials.

The general run of small fry were very earnest in their belief in Santa and often made grave and solemn professions of faith, despite the numerous copies shaking their bells on every Baltimore street corner. Parents were questioned thoroughly and often on the habits, diet and prejudices of Santa; their answers were received with awe. His demerits, if he had any, were never discussed for fear such discussion might suggest some similarity to the father of the inquirer. Happily, the evidence at the foot of the dazzling tree was sufficient to allay my doubts for many years.

One necessary preparation for Santa's coming was the cleaning of the chimney. Although we had a perfectly respectable and even impressive front door, Santa Claus hankered for this less conventional and devious entrance. Santa's whims were not to be ignored, so the chimney must be made ready. As a gesture to an honored craft, professional chimney sweeps were had in now and then, but most of the time and when there was no snow on the roof, my father did the job. He tied last year's Christmas tree to the end of the rope with a couple of sash weights on it. The whole bundle was dropped down the chimney and dragged through the flue until the voices below, stifled with soot, complained, "It's clean enough now."

We children prepared for Christmas by writing letters to Santa. Often whole pages of these letters were printed in the newspapers. Although it began as a public service, the custom helped to sell newspapers, for children importuned their parents to buy the paper until their letters appeared.

Before long, letters of facetious purpose began to appear from obviously bogus sources. The most frail and anemic girl would find herself the author of a request for boxing gloves, and the class bruiser would find his name under a printed plea for crocheted garters. Such letters were usually hatched by groups rather than by a single conspirator, and their secret identity was kept well. A grandmother of my acquaintance is still on the scent of the penman who urged a replacement for her dentures; she was the district's champion magpie.

Parents often encouraged nosy offspring to write Santa Claus in the hope of relieving themselves of endless questioning. As some of this correspondence came from those not too familiar with the alphabet, Santa Claus had to be a very sharp fellow to decipher the script and read their messages. My great quandary about the letters I shipped off to Santa was whether he received my missives. During personal visits to the old fellow on his throne, I detected a memory in chaos. Santa did not remember or could not recall exactly what was in my letter or whether he received it.

Perhaps one of Santa's brownies had not been paying attention to his work? Perhaps the delivery of my letters had been tampered with? I was never fully satisfied with Santa's responses to my questions, and I worried that I might not receive the presents I so earnestly requested. Even if Santa seemed to forget my letter, he always remembered to caution me to mend my ways before December 25. I would search my soul for the slanted testimony Santa could have spotted in my letters or for the slight frauds I had practiced as my own character witness.

While I was writing letters to Santa, the neighborhood patrolman prepared for Christmas by moving all disturbances indoors. The obstreperous were not arrested and transported at public expense, but gently handed through the front door of some friend or kin. Occasionally this arm of the law reached into the kitchen of certain homes for holiday refreshment, while other homes were entered only with a search warrant or a coroner.

At times during this season, the policeman had to deliver some male in a "fainting condition" to the nearest branch of his clan. In this case, the officer usually told us children "to clear out" and "give him air." Adults resorted to a terminology a child found very confusing. I heard such patients pronounced, and by experts no less, as anything from "wearing a lovely soch" to "fairly well starched." I could see nothing lovely or starched. What, I wondered, made the victim smell like the solution used to ignite plum pudding?

This same humane constable had to be on the lookout for another seasonal client, the family relative. At Christmas, our difficult relative was released from the sanatorium in order to visit us. Although he never arrived empty-handed, he was fortunate to arrive at all. He was usually very drunk by the time he neared our house and needed the cooperation of this sympathetic policeman to reach our door safely.

On one occasion this relative made it to the stoop of a house three doors from my family's home in the company of a huge live turkey. With difficulty, he held the turkey by one leg. Now any turkey can be excused for having a natural distaste for Christmas and everything connected with it, but this bird was of particularly nasty and unsociable traits. Judging from the turmoil, this turkey must have had a long record of mayhem.

The poor policeman was trying to get both the turkey and my relative to our house. By using the tactics prescribed for those resisting arrest, this foot soldier attempted to subdue the turkey, but to no avail. Besides being perverse of temper, this strutting monster was a champion dodger. Fortunately, word reached my home that a windfall was on its way, and we went to land the turkey in a body. As for the rescue of our relative, nature took its course. Mother processed the turkey, and her in-law was forgiven, with a warning against such antics again.

This particular in-law was a favorite of mine, and I was willing to overlook any of his caprices. During his stay with us, he did prodigies on the harmonica to amuse me. When his time was up and he had to return to the hospital in the hills, I howled after him in a heartrending manner and remained depressed for at least an hour.

The approach of Christmas was proclaimed with holly, visitors, letters to Santa, miniature gardens and special foods. From an upper window in every home in Union Square hung turkeys, geese and guinea hens "for seasoning," for want of refrigerators, and to deny poverty. Nobody in the commonwealth was going to admit to being too poor to buy some sort of fowl appropriate to the feast.

From the ovens, bakers turned out cookies with a rich taste of fennel, which had been hardened to the right crispness. At the grocers, fruits and nuts began to abound, and candy appeared in cargoes larger than the usual "cent's worth." The approach of Christmas was proclaimed from the scullery, which began to smell as though the entire product of the Spice Islands had exploded at the kitchen door. Christmas even came to the hen-house, for more eggs were ordered than would ever be eaten.

THOSE WHO ENTERTAINED US

7 Those Who Entertained Us

AMONG THE PLEASURES of the Christmas season was the
annual visit of Alec and Hilda. Both were in the full vigor
of their youth and of their love, which as far as I know,
never faltered. Mr. Willie met Alec and Hilda while they were
performing at an annual Harvest Festival. Alec and Hilda had
played a bride and groom in a rustic wedding scene, which was
the climax of the festival's stage spectacle. After endless re-
hearsals for their scenes, Alec and Hilda shifted parts from the
stage to real life and married.

Physically, Alec was one of the strongest and handsomest men I ever met. He had blonde hair and a noble face that Parisifal, the knight of the Round Table, might have envied. Starting as a cooper's apprentice he had become the designer and maker of nautical cabinets and finally an office-furniture manufacturer.

Not quite a head shorter than Alec, Hilda was also blonde, with a clear tan complexion, small brown eyes, a pleasant round face and an athletic figure. She started her working career as a bobbin girl in a shirt factory, a station just a shade more exaulted than that of a drudge in an orphan asylum. For better or worse, folks were caste-conscious in those days and very fine lines of social distinction were drawn by those not in the social register. The driver of a garbage cart, for example, received eight dollars a week for self and horse and regarded himself as above the lamplighter, who received only twelve dollars per month.

When Hilda and Alec came to visit at Christmas, they always reminisced about their acting days in the Harvest Festival, particularly their final performance. On that night, the play's manager came on stage in a military costume with a spiked helmet. While stagehands behind him dismantled a monument of fruit, he began to give a fierce political speech.

As he spoke, temptation gripped the stage crew. They could not resist shooting a few stray grapefruits at each other. The audience loved it. A serious speech was turned into a farce by their snickers, but the manager continued his patriotic soliloquy. Meanwhile, on a catwalk above the speaker, an unidentified man adjusted more scenery. Intentionally or not, this worker impaled a cantaloupe on the spike of the manager's helmet. At this, the howls of the audience reached a level loud enough to attract the police. The curtain came down on what was to be the last performance of this innocent festival; its demise was hastened by World War I and a notable experiment.

That night Mr. Willie found the hand that aimed the cantaloupe. He almost shook it off, for my father's universal love of mankind could not be stretched to include the manager in the helmet. The hand belonged to Alec. Every Christmas the

memory of this episode was evoked, while my parents and Hilda and Alec exploded with laughter.

At the request of Mr. Willie and Miss Katie, Hilda played the piano and she and Alec sang. They bowed slowly and formally before each number and at each burst of applause; they brought all the gravity of a sedate concert to our front room. By being their natural selves, Alec and Hilda were better entertainers at our house than they were behind the festival's footlights. They ate, drank, performed, and listened to the recitations of us children, who showed promise as wind machines at a tender age.

Christmas music was the instrument of my victory over a great fear of brass bands. During my youngest years, my brothers and I would hide under the nearest bed whenever we heard the sound of a brass band. I believed their tremendous sound was caused by a monster slamming down the lid of a vast box, and I feared being caught by this horror and being buried in the box. These wild fears came, I believe, from the fact that most of the brass bands I saw in my childhood were at the heads of funeral processions. For me, a brass band meant death.

The first assault to be heard was the crash and thump, the veritable earthquake of percussion from the brass drum and cymbals with a feeble and infrequent bray of brass. As my family never lived more than a city block from the main route to half a dozen graveyards, I was constantly seeing funeral corteges. If the deceased was an important person, a brass band was mandatory. Such processions were the signal for the suspension of work in shops and stores. For my mother, Miss Katie, a funeral train meant the prompt desertion of hearth and home to join the mob following the band to the cemetery.

The music that flooded the air on Christmas Eve finally ended my distaste and uneasiness with brass bands. At a local church, a contingent of brass and woodwinds played carols from a balcony near the top of a church spire. Their beautiful sound was enchanting, and the use of these band music instruments as prayer bells overcame my terror.

To discover what amused others at Christmas, I have talked to many about their favorite memories and activities. One friend who happened to be a descendent of a slave brought up an activity I had given little thought to. This man's idea of a good Christmas was to sit in front of a good fire, crack nuts, and throw the shells into the flames. The shells produced a small fireworks display and added to the pleasure of this pastime.

Music boxes were another feature of Christmas that I took for granted, though they are fondly remembered by others. At the height of their popularity, music boxes were set going at dusk to welcome the man of the house on his return from a hard day at the shop; often their melodious tinkle could be heard from slightly opened windows. Made by master craftsmen, their tone was true and their cabinetwork perfect.

In an era before such wicked novelties as the ukulele and the speakeasy, my contemporaries and I were amused by very simple things, such as observing the enterprises and seasonal conduct of our friends. In my neighborhood, and I say it sorrowing, everybody drank. The drinking was usually in moderation, in very steady moderation, but drink they did. Christmas certainly was not the season for "swearing off." At Christmas, the supply of liquor was most abundant.

Upon occasion a beverage surprised its drinker and caused swift and heady results. In such cases, the gentlemen or the ladies were never drunk. If they were in need of assistance and hilarious, they were "jolly"; if they were surly or spiteful, they were "afflicted." The afflicted sometimes became public nuisances and were arrested and tried strictly. The thesis was that if a person did not expand charitably, he had no right to succumb to the influence. All public officers frowned on such dangerous ingrates whose attitude did an injustice to the treasures of nature. Angry drunks were sent into isolation in the clink.

The ministrations of saloon keepers and bartenders were regarded as healthful, soothing, and healing, and they were often given the title of "Professor" or "Doctor." The Germans had an endless list of honorifics for those who presided at the spigots; their titles rose in proportion to the aristocratic appearance of the tapster. There was a nobility about their calling that tempted the poor to claim them as cousins. Tavern owners themselves were often addressed as "Pap" or "Daddy," and a widow who perpetuated the philanthropy of her late husband was sometimes called "Mammy."

In return for their titles of respect, tavern keepers conferred honorifics of political and social importance on their patrons. Even an irregular client like my father was named "Colonel." Father usually dropped in on taverns only at Christmas to sample and compliment the owners on the seasonal improvement of the *wurstle* in their free bar lunch. The free lunch, which helped many a man through college, was diligently policed against the undeserving even at Christmas. There was a gentlemen's agreement to be uniformly observed at any season — "Thou shalt earn thy bread!"

I saw very little of the adult assemblies inside saloons, unless the view was from under the swinging doors during the mild weather. As a rule, bartenders had a genteel and sagacious air about them and were kindly condescending to children. Children, however, were not welcome in bars and were either bribed to vacate with steamed crabs and pretzels or just threatened to "git."

At some other adult functions, children were tolerated for a time and then dismissed. One ladies' group held an annual winter taffy pull and invited the local children. As my experience with them was brief, I cannot speak with great authority. I was asked in an "itty-bitty" voice, "Does the little boy like the taffy pull?" I thought it was messy and said so. For this indiscretion, I was thrown out and never invited again.

Sometimes I was present at adult gatherings by accident or by not being noticed. I happened upon the antics of a local family who was infatuated with their donkey. For reasons not obvious, they considered this beast exceptionally gifted and decided that their donkey should see their Christmas tree. To get the donkey into the house, the grownups coddled and coaxed, and pushed and dragged that donkey up the steps, across the

porch, through the kitchen, and between the rooms to reach the tree in the parlor.

These neighbors excused their whimsy by surmising that any donkey ought to have a hereditary appreciation of Christmas. After all, was not a donkey part of the first Christmas?

By the time I was in first grade, my amusement program during the holidays advanced. I was left on my own to play with three or four buddies. Together, we would wander six to eight blocks from our district to look at Christmas displays. Since we were not anxious to attract the attention of unknown policemen, we did not select the same course twice. In these distant places, we would inspect the Christmas trees and gardens of total strangers.

Whenever we spied a lower branch of a tree with a ball or two and some tinsel framed in a front window, we would climb up to the front porch window for a better look. We would peer inside these windows and make invidious comparisons, always deciding that this garden or tree was not quite as nice as the ones in our district. Even if a display was much better, we never admitted it. Santa Claus was always in a position to retaliate, so we never spoke of his treatment to us in terms short of perfection. We did, however, take mental note of those articles we admired most to make sure that Santa would bring them for us next Christmas.

We considered such tours public amusement, since these exhibitors were not known to us. Sometimes when the owners of the houses saw strange children's faces at their windows, they invited us in for a closer inspection. None that I recall ever complained or called an officer. In fact, our peeping flattered them. Many folks offered us cakes or candy, but my mother had an edict against eating in strange homes. Miss Katie's x-ray eyes could detect off-the-reservation confections in my innards, so I always declined these foreign goodies.

Our public entertainment also included trudging fifteen city blocks to view the windows of the various stores. I preferred the toy stores; one featured mechanical tops, another carpenter's tools, a third model boats. As I was intrigued by my reflection in the bells of cornets, trombones and French horns, I also visited the music stores at Christmas while passing over windows full of dry goods, shoes and tobacco.

The mental picture I formed of these window displays was quite indelible. If a store window displayed a regiment of lead soldiers one year, I quickly spotted any variation in the arrangement the next. My friends and I gazed at these displays and wondered where all the miles of ribbon and tons of tinsel were stored after Christmas. Silver paper, gold stars and red ribbon were treasures we thought too precious to throw away.

PARTIES, BRASS BANDS AND SINGERS

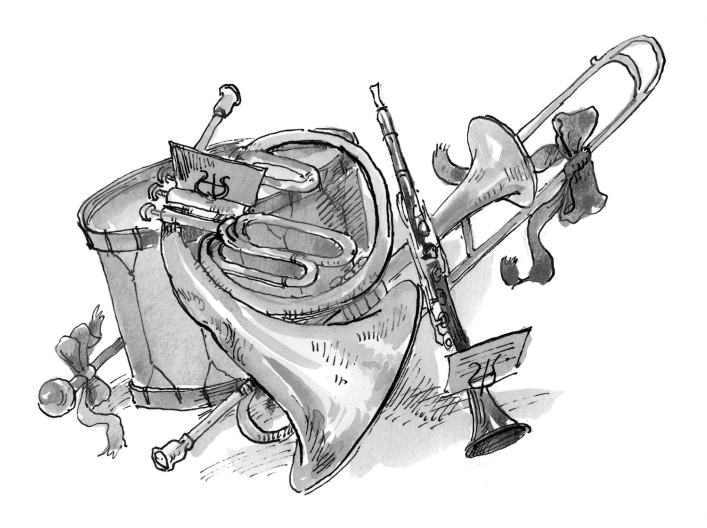

8 Parties, Brass Bands and Singers

No matter what pleasant diversion Christmas offered me in the way of cultural displays the best pastime was watching the antics of my elders. Usually my parents entertained their friends singly or in very small groups, but once in a while they gave a large Christmas party. Although I was not able to observe each person at a party as well as I could when they visited individually, I gave my attention to the most outstanding ones. By outstanding, I mean the guests who distinguished themselves with their monkeyshines.

Most of these parties took place in the large kitchen of my family's first home—the home where Mr. Willie and Miss Katie moved when they married ninety years ago and the home where all the children were born. Party invitations were oral and were extended to married aunts and uncles, to courting nephews and nieces, and to friends. Miss Katie used to say, "We are going to have a party," for the expression "to give" or "to throw" was not then current. Usually the date was set for the Saturday between Christmas and New Year's. No great preparation was necessary. The main ingredients for a successful gathering were food, drink and piano players.

Since Miss Katie had a cousin who had attended the conservatory and had made many friends before his expulsion, she had no trouble lining up several piano players for an evening. A reserve of musicians was advisable, for a piano player might appear in an odd state after playing in an afternoon wedding reception or might collapse after playing a strenuous polka. Our piano players were usually male and often brought their wives or sweethearts for the evening. Money was scarce for musicians, but they all enjoyed a good meal at Miss Katie's buffet.

Miss Katie filled the sideboard in the living room with ham, roast beef, chicken, breads, cake and ice cream. For many, a party could not take place without cake and ice cream! At Christmas, our kitchen shelves were outrageously encumbered with cake, and Miss Katie thought parties were a fine way to unload this overabundance. To make room for dancing in the kitchen, the kitchen table and stove were taken out, and a line of chairs was placed along one wall for resting between polkas.

The parties got underway demurely enough. Couples arrived, took off their "duds" and conversed. The ladies sat or helped Miss Katie, and the gentlemen stood. Mr. Willie introduced those he thought were not known to each other and isolated the uninvited. When the music began, nearly all the guests danced with vigor and without intermission.

Until midnight, the party progressed merrily. At that hour, many began to think about going home in order to appear rested and innocent of all carousing at church the next morning. Excesses were frowned upon, and no one wanted to give evidence of drinking too much or partying too long. The activities slowed down, and the guests began to put the house back to order. The dishes were washed and put away, the furniture was arranged properly, and the stove was returned to the kitchen. Cleaning up was more arduous than preparing for a party, and appreciative guests were always kind enough to lend a hand.

One man's presence played an important part in a party's success; he was a champion of misfortune named Joe. If any mischance was to be dished out, Joe was the first in line. He was a man with a stoop, of medium build, and of unsteady gait. He wore his eyes half-closed in a face that was a cross between Bacchus and prehistoric man, but not quite bad enough to frighten children. Joe was unfortunate by heredity, by instinct, and by destiny. Never a young or a strong man, his death was predicted annually for half a century. He loved his wives excessively and was married and widowed twice in three years.

His only known venture into steady employment was with a low-grade mortician in an extremely healthy district. Joe aspired briefly to this profession, because it seemed the cleanest and the least laborious livelihood at a time when most men labored in sweat and grime. Due to a failure to master the conservative appearance necessary in the undertaking business, he was dismissed. At one interment, he appeared with his shirttail hanging and at another, his cravat waved from the back of his neck.

Joe was brilliant in another field; he was a born minstrel. His songs entranced me by the hour. Some, which were not for a child to understand, caused adults to whoop, crackle and flop in an hysterical manner. The source of his musical education was a mystery, but Joe was a master. He made stringed instruments out of discarded odds and ends and played them with skill. Besides this unique mastery, he displayed a veritable wizardry on the glockenspiel bequeathed him by an admiring percussionist, executed prodigies on the piano, and was in demand as an engineer of rowdy soirees in private residences. He traveled from house to house and unveiled his talents to the appreciative.

Joe was on to all party tricks and games and could make almost any crowd create its own amusement, enter into the spirit of it, and enjoy themselves. Once he suggested a community sing of "Schnitzel bank"; this game required a list of items to be named in order. At one of our parties the audience was familiar with the articles but vague about the order of naming them. Joe unrolled a cream-colored blind off its roller, and for a visual aid, drew the articles on the blind. Miss Katie, who was very precise about the integrity of her household, did not object or complain. She simply replaced the blind the next morning.

Joe's presence at a party had one drawback; his talent attracted a large number of uninvited, impolite fans. If they got inside, these fans gave way to infamous conduct. They were not satisfied with admiring the ornamental bowl on the sideboard, but also took nasty liberties with its contents. They pronounced perfectly good eggnog "negus," and made themselves completely disliked. These gatecrashers greatly upset Joe, who would not play until the rabble was thrown out. Finally these wild fans upset him so that he abandoned his public and retired from his form of concert work.

I only saw Joe twice after his retirement: once he appeared to prevent his third wife from burying a derelict in his stead and once at my mother's funeral.

The Christmas Party

Joe's wife identified a man found dead of a broken neck at the foot of a long staircase as her lost mate. The mistake was excusable as the corpse's face was unshaven, discolored, and bloated just like Joe's. The coroner released the body to the family, the undertaker prepared it, and a church funeral was arranged. The evening before the funeral, Joe walked into the embalmer's display room and corrected the error. What a mistake, and what a conversation the undertaker and Joe must have had!

Whether at a funeral held for him or someone else, Joe seemed out of place. When Joe came out of retirement one last time to attend my mother's remains to the grave, our oyster-loving dentist, by mistake, told him to beat it. He thought Joe was a vagrant. Later the dentist claimed that, although he had frequented our home for twenty years, he did not remember Joe. We all felt bad that Joe, our friend and good glockenspiel player, had been so shabbily treated.

One public display, which I cannot omit, was the brass band created through the efforts and imagination of a struggling barber. A short, slight, and wiry man, he was indefatigable. His haircuts were fifteen cents and shaves ten in an inconspicuous shop called "The Tonsorial Parlor." This barber had a price list of singes, shampoos, facial massages, and other miscellaneous groomings never called for except by a man out courting or out of his mind. On the wall facing the two chairs in the shop were these signs, "Cash Today, Credit Tomorrow" and "No Politics Talked in This Shop."

On Saturday nights, he devoted his time to shaving old men who could no longer trust themselves with a straight razor. Each of these customers had his own private cup and brush, which was stored on a wall rack. The shaving bee was done in an assembly-line manner. The barber shaved, while one of his ten sons lathered. The waiting customers sat on straight-backed chairs in two rows like a jury box and often overflowed outside to the steps and pavement. As far as I can remember, there was never any close vocal harmony emanating from this shop, but there were sounds of brass. The barber would interrupt the shaving of a customer to yell at some unseen instrumentalist, "You missed that B-flat again!"

Supposedly, this prolific man had ten sons and put each one to use in his brass band. I say supposedly, because some folks believed he selected his sons from reform school on the basis of the instruments they could play. This theory springs from the fact that nobody ever saw his wife or ever heard of any christenings at the house. By whatever means, this barber formed his own brass band, which practiced in the rooms behind and above the shop. Fortunately the band played well enough not to be bombarded with complaints.

Now and then the band marched in small parades and played at funerals, but their talents were displayed full blast every New Year's Eve. The evening began with a substantial supper for the band, their friends and well wishers. After eating, the band members plus thirty or forty comrades emerged from the barbershop and stood in reverent formation on the pavement outside for the rest of the activities. A capricious and ancient man acted as master of ceremonies and introduced a number of nonentities and the principal speaker, a seasoned blatherskite in tie and tails and a paperhanger by trade.

Whether the lecturer was finished or not, the band took over at 11:50 p.m. and launched into "Auld Lang Syne." The music began in a meditative manner at first and then, after a verse and chorus, shifted to a *tempo di marcia* and off they strutted down the street and around the block. While they paraded down nearby streets and played the old year out and the new year in, bemused neighbors draped themselves out of windows, porches and doors. Some waved flares to encourage the marchers and get a better look at the ceremony. Although the parade was held without a permit, no interference came from the local policeman, who looked the other way after receiving a good free meal.

The New Year's Eve Brass Band

The midnight recital of a brass band was accepted as part of the proprieties due the Christmas season in our neighborly community. No one seemed disturbed, and in some families, children were made to take a nap during the day in order to stay up at night to see and hear the parade. The band was the local and unique custom of Union Square.

Other public entertainment came my way. Occasionally, the managers of theaters handed Mr. Willie a ticket or two for the Saturday matinee at their houses. The first of these that my maturity justified seeing was "The Old Homestead," a melodrama. Because everybody else in the family had seen it, I saw it as part of my education as a gentleman. The theater's atmosphere was elegant and muted. Red velvet curtains were arranged at the tops of the boxes and held at the sides with reels of gold rope. The plush of the seats, and there was an ocean of it, must have been the material for the robes of kings. With the gold leaf on the fluted columns, grills and lighting fixtures, I decided a palace must look just like a vaudeville house.

On one visit, the maiden lady in the seat beside me managed to stuff me with "old-fashions," chocolate drops then in great favor with those completely unconscious of calories, while a male quartet of farm hands sang on stage. They sang "The Old Oaken Bucket" and "Jingle Bells" in what I thought was an artistic and tasteful manner. When they performed "Where is my Wand'ring Boy Tonight," tears began to fall in the audience. To increase the pathos, half of the stage was blacked out, while the other half was occupied with a tableau of the wandering boy at a bar gazing off into space. His foot was on the rail and he held a lit cigar and an enormous glass of beer. In fact, the glass was so large that is seemed that such a weak and thin boy could never have lifted it. This scene left me cold for two reasons. One was that all the children in our neighborhood had beer with their meals. The second was the obvious fake emphasis on the size of the mug or seidel. Even I realized that any young man working his way to ruin would use a handier instrument.

This stage performance was a course leading to the dignity of being a spectator at a minstrel show, which preceded Christmas by a few days. The minstrel group was composed of city, state and federal employees recruited from the City Hall, courthouse, post office, and various bars. This convivial lot was out to raise money to buy coal for the city's poor, because the proper agency faced a hard winter without funds. Although they had a tall hula dancer who excited considerable attention and merriment, the cast was all male. In an act called "General Delivery and General Nuisance," the second tenor pushed his 300-pound partner in a baby carriage. All sang expansively and with perfect control; I have yet to encounter their equals.

During the Christmas season, these minstrel singers were in demand in church choirs around the city. Mr. Willie managed to get about a dozen singers to our house at least one night out of the year, and he left our doors and windows open for the benefit of an appreciative audience of near neighbors. As a rule, they went through their repertoire in an orderly manner and called it a night.

The city's minstrel men brought much pleasure to our Christmas season. Their settled and exceptional voices were far superior to the groups who distilled their precious harmonies, as Mr. Willie opined, "too near and too often." I doubt if any of these minstrel singers survive today, but between forty and fifty years was an average age then. As their services were gratis and they did not depend on singing for a living, the minstrel company was organized quickly and seemed to fall apart fast. Their songs were made "for he-man quartetting," and they would have had no truck with crooning, if they had ever heard it.

Up until now I have confined myself to those happenings at home and in the environs, with the exception of the private tours to snoop at trees and gardens some distance from home. One longer journey we made officially was to visit the workhouse for incorrigible young males. The officer in charge was well known to us: He often threatened us with an unhappy future if we did not soon show signs of conversion. One of the statements of this overbearing official was, "I did not see you at Sunday School last Sunday." Naturally, since we were of different religions, he did not. So we were not in awe of him, in spite of the stories of fancy tortures visited on little boys, once inside the dark vaults of his domain.

Yet one aspect of the place impressed us. The annual workhouse Christmas Garden, around the foot of an enormous tree that stood at the concourse where the tiers joined, was more elaborate and up-to-date than that in any of our homes. It had been fabricated by some of the best craftsmen in the city, who donated both time and material to making it one of the most resplendent exhibits of its kind. It was so good that visiting urchins secretly longed to be made inmates of the place until Christmas was over for the year. As usual, the layout included steam locomotives propelled by a highly volatile fuel, and these managed to blow up at least once a season. Since the "wards" of the commonwealth were never allowed that near to the trains, injuries were invariably sustained by the faculty. This hazard started Mr. Willie on a crusade. Although not a drinking man himself, his heart bled for the faculty, for he concluded that the nearest they ever came to alcohol was a sniff from a passing toy engine. The crusade died a natural death when he learned that management and staff were free to take any thirst-abating measures necessary to remedy their scorched condition—outside the walls. This was a necessary precaution to protect the minors within, since many of them needed no lessons as cracksmen, and were already thieves of distinction. At our age, the needs of the faculty hardly bothered us, but we were a bit puzzled by our observation that the way of the transgressor was not so hard after he was brought to book. Nobody on the outside had such a tree or such a garden!

All over our section of town, in this era, the urge to be gregarious caused many small lodges and social clubs to sprout. They held their orgies indoors, without noticeable hullabuloo, and apart from their existence being known, they managed to remain secret societies.

The night after Christmas, unless it fell on Sunday, was designated for the "Musical Mask" of the "Amity Brethren, Jericho Nest #23." It was not held on Sunday evenings, inasmuch as the members were gainfully employed that night of the week and so prevented from congregating. As I understood it, the "Amity" had nothing to do with a policy of good feeling among members, although they were people of great loyalty. In fact, as regards treasurers, good feeling "had been read out of the lodge" at an early date in the lodge's existence. Treasurers were excluded from any and all good will because of the prudent brothers' rank distrust of these officers. So, if they were never unanimous in their election of a treasurer, they surely were in their suspicions of one and all. Hence this tale is told not about one, but about *two* treasurers.

The lodge was named after Amity Terrace because "it sounded like a nice name." It was, in truth, the nickname for a notorious and unsanitary alley whose denizens got—and deserved—more pacifying from the police than any comparable area in a seaport of that size.

"Jericho Nest" was chosen because it fairly jumped with biblical dignity. "Jericho" had stood the test of time.

"Number 23" as far as I could learn, did not argue the existence of twenty-two previous foundations, but was chosen because of its affinity to "skidoo" or "vamoose," a practice well known to the brethren, who were required to be fugitive on occasion. All hoped to be equally fleet of foot or prompt of departure when their own need arose.

Annually, at Christmas, they relaxed the dignity of the lodge with a masked ball. They managed to rent or otherwise have put at their disposal the vacant loft of a building contractor. It was a huge place with floor space almost equal to that of a small armory, with a good solid floor, not too smooth, and within walls that were almost sound-proof. Here they pooled and plied their buffoonery in costume, to the strains of the banjo, corn fiddle and other unusual instruments. Exits were plentiful, and had to be, for such conservative routs were known to get out of hand, in which case immediate access to the wide open spaces was of the essence for noncombatants. Through one of these exits, during one Christmas frolic, the treasurer disappeared. His brethren paid him no mind, however; after all, vanishing was a tomfoolery often indulged in by treasurers. Moreover, since this one was dressed as Santa Claus, it could very well have been part of the program. At any rate, his disappearance escaped the notice of the revelers, who were giving their all to the dance.

However, although not present in the hall, the police did note this disappearance. (They remained outside, as a rule, to take care of likely casualties, gate-crashers, and any who might return with reinforcements after having been previously ejected.)

A patrolman on duty outside was curious to see Santa Claus, so essential a part of any Christmas function, casually desert the festivities. Later, a constable spotted him, whiskers and all, appropriating a few things in a nearby warehouse. That is, he was at least making a selection of merchandise and piling up the selections near the door to the loading platform. What his plan might be was not entirely clear. One thing *was* clear to the constable; namely, that he could by no means associate the face behind those whiskers with the North Pole. Sociable contact with the constabulary not being among "Santa's" plans at that time, he "just lit right out!"

Meanwhile, something else developed within the loft, where the revelers were in full vigor. The ex-treasurer, dressed as Mephisto, had been at dalliance with a lady, who backed him into the switchboard. This panel being obsolete, his crushing contact caused it to arc and to ignite the rear, lower fringe of the cloak he was wearing. Soon the outfit began to smoke and smoulder, and then glow. As soon as the ex-treasurer became aware of it, instinct indicated a short-cut to a roll in the nearest snow. Here the laws of physics must have worked against him, for the fleetness of his sprinting only served to fan the combustion he carried along. No doubt the pain at the seat of his discomfort distracted him, for once outdoors he forgot what he came for. Instead of diving for the snow bank, he began to leap and howl and perform all sorts of ludicrous whirling maneuvers. Finally, he darted off in one direction in earnest. Through a wrong turn or some other accident, he took the same path as the current treasurer, who had just been surprised in the warehouse. By uncanny coincidence, he was only a few moments behind, in the identical line of determined departure. In other words, he was between the police and the pursued.

The chase headed through Amity Terrace. Now, since an intinerant cremation was a matter for the fire department, the police lost interest in it after it cleared the thoroughfare, and began to regard it as no affair of theirs. At the rate they were all running, it was about time for the man on the third beat removed to worry over it. The effect was quite startling to the neighbors around the thoroughfare, who suddenly became forced witnesses. When they saw a racing Santa Claus pursued by a devil with a smoking bottom — and the police — they thought the whole medieval demonology had been turned loose in the neighborhood against a time-honored symbol of Christmas. Hell was definitely invading their retreat! Realizing that the proper location for all decent believers was at some distance elsewhere, they all managed to get to some other place without another moment's hesitation.

Somewhere, there should be an old medical record of the treatment of a youth for blisters, burns or even a possible skin graft. There should also be records of a costumer who never got back the regalia for a would-be Lucifer. In that time and place, a footrace with the law was too common to invite comment, but what happened to the tennants in the path of flight is something landlords and other creditors tried their utmost to find out. The whole block was deserted before dawn. Even the sick and senile decamped. The evacuation was unprecedented for thoroughness and dispatch. In fact, the first and fastest slum clearance in the city had been accomplished. And this miracle was deemed — by all those who were not left with unpaid debts — to be the best Christmas gift of this bountiful Santa, caught in the act of helping himself.

HONORING CHRISTMAS

9 Honoring Christmas

THANKS TO MY ELDERS, Christmas was a triple abundance of food, toys and amusements. Trees and toys made such an impression on my childish brain that the memory of Christmas menus is less than vivid. In my neighborhood, the emphasis was on great quantities of food. Any parents feeding a child less than three thousand calories at one sitting was courting public consternation and a business call from the asylum. A child on the loose was presumed underfed, and any hausfrau, cook, baker and confectioner was at liberty to ambush and stuff the youngster. This fate befell little boys more than girls, but none seemed to suffer from it. According to community standards back then, the average man should be a formidable trencherman or be mourned as an unfortunate weakling.

When my family didn't eat Christmas dinner at home, we went to my paternal grandmother's for the big meal. Because she had only a little tree on a table and no toys and trains, I was always a bit disappointed to be going. At grandmother's, the guest list included homesick immigrants and relatives, rich and poor. For the sake of the "greenhorns," the dinner included corned beef, cabbage and potatoes, all boiled in the same pot. In addition, hams, turkeys, tongues, beef roasts, spinach dishes with hard-boiled eggs, mince pies and fruitcakes were brought by the guests. Appetites were in inverse proportion to the size of the contributions.

Many of grandmother's guests claimed to have left their watches home and never knew when it was time to go home. To signal that the meal was over, Jim, our friend and the ex-policeman, concocted a bowl of liquid refreshment with a vanilla aroma. All adults were invited to "have a taste before leaving." Unfortunately these guests became enamored of Jim's company and his bowl and didn't take the hint to drink and depart. Finally, the job of getting rid of the stragglers fell to two muscular brothers whom grandmother had brought over from Erin, Ireland. With a few words, the dear boys cleared the premises. They never failed in their gratitude to the old lady and kept her in whiskey with which to say her prayers all of her days. After the guests left, grandmother went back to her prayers, and we went home to swoon in the presence of our toys and the tree.

Many Christmas dinners took place at my own home. Miss Katie's dinner was a baked affair in a two-temperature stove. The turkey was usually stuffed with a combination of sausage and chestnuts, which was the family favorite over sage and oyster dressing. Since frozen vegetables had not yet become a part of our lives, the vegetables were home-canned string beans, peas and tomatoes seasoned with fresh onions and croutons. In my family, sauerkraut was not served with turkey, but there were always side dishes of coleslaw, pickles, homemade bread and biscuits.

To my father, soup was a mark of poverty and was outlawed from our table. Since fresh fruit juice was not readily available, cider was the beverage for a Christian child's Christmas dinner. Desserts were an important part of this feast and were plentiful. Christmas rated a plum pudding; New Year's got a mince pie. Between meals, fruitcakes, which had been curing since autumn and included at least four varieties, were available to all.

In later years, the Christmas menu was changed to include filet mignon with mushrooms and wine, followed by fresh ham and vegetables, mince pie with champagne, and fruitcake with liqueurs. But in those early days, nothing alcoholic was served. The guests at our table were mostly unmarried in-laws, whose equilibrium and judgment was easily disturbed by alcohol.

Nobody who had his own home went visiting on Christmas Day. Occasional stragglers, however, happened over to our house on their way home from church. These unexpected visitors were left to us children to entertain, because my mother was directing a major operation in the kitchen, and father was singing in his quartet at the city jail. We children occupied these guests by ignoring their small talk and by pointing out the stupendous virtues of the gifts left to us by St. Nick.

One person who always showed up was Julie, a spinster. Having nowhere to go, Julie and her mechanical dwarf would come to our house on Christmas night. For our entertainment, the dwarf would be hitched to a series of pulleys turned by the motor in our miniature garden. When the motor was turned on, the dwarf sawed wood in a manner that threatened to outdistance the whole lumber industry of the great Northwest.

Julie was a teetotaler and in her youth had been a disciple of Carrie Nation, the agitator for temperance in America. Nature had granted Julie few favors, but one was the gift of copious tears. Julie cherished this gift, and her mourning was of real concert caliber. If grief was cultivated by tears, Julie did what she could to make grief immortal. On a Christmas evening, Julie would sob at the sight of her dwarf sawing away for dear life. Her outpourings threatened to submerge the entire neighborhood.

Since Julie's howlings eventually threatened to ruin my family's Christmas evening, my father developed a technique to send Julie on her way. (He used this same method to get rid of uncles, mostly honorary, who itched to manipulate the train and other operating gadgets in the garden.) Removing the motor's batteries, Mr. Willie would tell Julie that the dwarf, the train, and the rest of the team of performers in our miniature garden were tired and had to rest. He would then help Julie to her hat and coat and hold our front door open for her.

After Julie and all other stray guests were gone, my siblings and I could finally concentrate on the uninterrupted joy of having our toys to ourselves. I had looked forward to this opportunity for a long, long time. Night had fallen, and every moment was precious.

My parents would sit on chairs and watch all of us children play on the floor with our new toys. They would speak softly and smile to each other. Finally my father would speak, asking a question which he asked every Christmas for forty years. "Katie, would you like a glass of wine?" Miss Katie was then treated to a glass of her own vintage from the previous summer's grape harvest. This ritual signaled nine o'clock, which was the anniversary, to the hour, of their engagement. Until my mother's death, father asked the same question every December 25th at 9 p.m. to commemorate their promise to each other.

While their memorable toast was being drunk, we children busily explored the possibilities of our new musical instruments. Drumming was out, because it might disturb the neighbors. Hammering or sawing with our new carpenter's tools was permitted, provided it was done quietly. When we had tired of making noise, we attempted something soothing and in keeping with the feast and the hour. Playing our reedy horns or toy flutes, we tried to coax simple melodies like "Home Sweet Home" or "Three Blind Mice" from our instruments.

On Christmas night in my earlier years, I would use my new toys to build imaginary but very patrician mansions, to make runs with tiny fire engines to make-believe fires, and to slay ferocious invisible animals with my popgun. After these games, I would try to remember the arrangement of all the gifts at my first sight of them. The fire engine hook and ladder had to be backed into its station house in a perfect line, the gun had to be restored to its position under the tree, and the imaginary animals had to be restored to life for the next day's hunt.

The late Christmas curfew had arrived, and we children had to go to bed. The last thing I was able to do was to look at the tree. The last picture I took to my dreams was the brilliant Joseph's coat of many colors which adorned it. Nothing could compare with the tree's beauty on Christmas night, not the ball park, not the theater, not the circus, and not even the fruit monument at the Harvest Festival.

The final ritual was father's dramatic reading of "A Visit from St. Nicholas." But that Christmas happened to somebody else. This Christmas happened to me, and I wanted it to stay.

"Children, Christmas is over now. Next Christmas is just about as far away as it can be." My parents' announcement was a sad one. Christmas was so bright and beautiful, and the people with it! I did not know it then, but later I learned that I was of the same mind as a certain character of Charles Dickens who, like all the folks I knew back then, "would honor Christmas in his heart and try to keep it all the year round."

Son of Catherine and William F. Stricker and descendant of General John Stricker, who led the land defense against British forces in 1814, WILLIAM F. STRICKER was born on November 3, 1903. Known as Will or Willy as a boy, Pete when he grew up, he lived in the rowhouse next door to that of H. L. Mencken, whose close friend he became. An altar boy who even then wanted to become a priest, he attended parochial schools before entering St. Charles College and St. Mary's Seminary. He then went to Rome, where he attended the North American College. Ordained a priest in 1929 while in Rome, he became in 1948 the first resident pastor of St. Bernadette's Parish, serving the people of east Silver Spring, Maryland. In 1959, Pope John XXIII raised him to the rank of Domestic Prelate.

Well known in the circles of statesmen and American presidents, with whom he lunched and conversed regularly, Monsignor Stricker's own parishioners knew him as a man of "disarming Mencken-like wit, with which he could readily puncture pomp and pretense. A student of literature and of his native Maryland, he often combined anecdotes or briefs from both in his sermons. It seemed, however, that Christmas brought out some of the pastor's fondest memories...."

His death on October 14, 1976 brought eulogies not only from his own parishioners, but from hundreds of others, including Lieutenant Governor Blair Lee III of Maryland, who remembered him as "clear-eyed, hard-headed, and a person who always told it like it was."

JOSEPH SHEPPARD, born in Owings Mills, Maryland in 1930, has always delighted in painting scenes of Baltimore life, and many of his murals adorn Baltimore buildings. He attended the Maryland Institute College of Art on a four-year scholarship, and later taught there, as well as at Dickinson College, Pennsylvania, where he was Artist-in-Residence. His paintings have brought him many prizes and awards, as well as commissions such as that for seven large murals to grace Baltimore's new police headquarters. His work hangs in many public and private collections throughout America and Europe. He has also published four books on figure-drawing that have been widely acclaimed. Married to sculptor Nina Akamu, he currently lives and maintains a studio in Florence, Italy, but returns to his beloved Baltimore each year.

Designed by Barbara Holdridge

Composed in Baskerville with Torino/Flair display by the
Service Composition Company, Baltimore, Maryland

Color separations produced by Capper, Inc.,
Knoxville, Tennessee

Printed on 80-pound Mead Matte text and Monadnock
Astrolite Fancy Finish end-papers by
Federated Lithographers—Printers, Inc.,
Providence, Rhode Island

Jacket printed by Rugby, Inc., Knoxville, Tennessee

Bound in Joanna Buckram cloth for the spine and Crown
Linen cloth for the sides
by Delmar Printing Company,
Charlotte, North Carolina

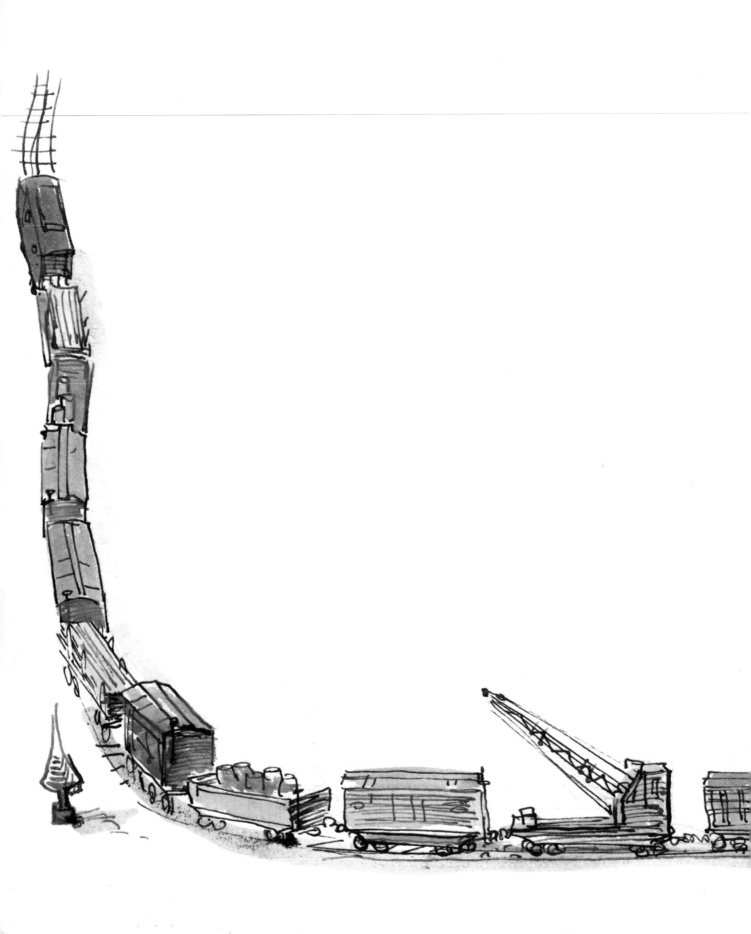